mac's year

1991

Cartoons from the *Daily Mail*

Stan McMurtry **mac**

Chapmans

To Janny

Chapmans Publishers Ltd
141–143 Drury Lane
London WC2B 5TB

First published by Chapmans 1991

© Stan McMurtry 1991

ISBN 1 85592 716 0

Printed and bound in Great Britain by
Clays Ltd, St Ives plc

In an experimental service, 11,000 chemists in popular coastal resorts offered holidaymakers pollution tests on Britain's seawater.

'Well? Speak up man! Is it safe?' *August 2*

As the Cold War drew to a close in newly united Europe, fresh dangers
loomed in the Middle East.

August 3

Unofficial strikes on North Sea oilrigs, combined with increasing nervousness about the situation in Kuwait, led to fuel shortages at home.

'It's his Lordship, M'lady – don't smoke near the swimming pool, he's filled it with petrol . . .' *August 7*

As the UN blockade on Iraq tightened, supplies began to run short.

'I suppose this means no pudding?' *August 12*

British forces built up in the Gulf at the traditional start of the grouse-shooting season.

'It says here it's the start of the LOUSE shooting season – surely that's a spelling mistake?' *August 14*

‘Honest broker’ King Hussein of Jordan flew to President Bush's holiday
home in an attempt to prevent a conflict which threatened to bankrupt
his country's ailing economy.

'Let me explain, Clancy – there are two Husseins, a goody and a baddy. The one you just threw out of
the window was the goody . . .' *August 16*

After 12 years as a BBC TV sports presenter, Green Party activist David Icke claimed that there was political motivation behind his dismissal following his high-profile stand against the poll tax.

'I think we've found David Icke's successor. He doesn't give a stuff for the environment and could be persuaded to pay his poll tax . . .' *August 17*

In occupied Kuwait 200 Britons were held hostage in the five-star Al-Mansur Melia hotel in Baghdad in an effort to delay an Allied assault.

'Iraq's brave and heroic leader strikes again!' *August 20*

When Saddam Hussein announced that 5000 Soviet workers would also be held hostage in Baghdad, Moscow revealed details of Iraq's chemical warfare weapons.

'Just one sniff and it drives a person to dribbling insanity – our glorious leader tested it himself . . .'

August 21

The Palace was outraged when candid photos of the Queen and Queen Mother stolen from the Royal Family's personal album were printed in European magazines.

'. . . and just how much is the nice gentleman from the Press paying you for this, William?' *August 23*

As multinational troops mustered on the Kuwait/Saudi border in preparation for Operation Desert Storm, temperatures in Britain soared into the eighties for the Bank Holiday weekend.

'I sure hope there's no action before Tuesday, Sarge – the Brits insist on having their Bank Holiday.'

August 27

As part of a £1.75 million appeal to build a 'gorillarium' at John Aspinall's Howlett's Zoo in Kent, his nine-month-old granddaughter Tansy posed for the press with playmate Sangha the baby gorilla.

'. . . and remember, Nicholas, when the babysitter says it's time for bed – no arguing.' *August 28*

After 113 days a verdict was reached in the Guinness trial. Heron International chief, Gerald Ronson, received a record £5 million fine and a year in jail.

'Well, if I was you, Fingers, I'd take his promise of a yacht and directorship of Heron International with a pinch of salt . . .' *August 30*

With the reality of war moving ever closer, it was announced that British women and children held hostage in Iraq would be released and evacuated to London.

'I'm sorry, men, but it's the only way I can think of to get us out of this mess . . .' *August 31*

As the hostage children landed at Heathrow, former US presidential candidate Jesse Jackson scooped up Stuart Lockwood, who had appeared on TV with Saddam Hussein. In Blackpool, Norman Willis opened the TUC conference.

'Forget those photos with Saddam Hussein and Jesse Jackson! This is the big one, kid! How would you like to be cuddled by Norman Willis at the TUC conference?' *September 4*

Parliament was recalled during the summer recess to consider the Gulf crisis.

'Come on, Henry. We can't disembowel, behead and nuke every single Arab just because your holiday has been interrupted . . .' *September 6*

Interviewed on TV-am the Prime Minister, 64, declared that she intended to remain head of the Conservative Party until she was 70 as UN sanctions increased their grip in the Middle East.

'How much food did you say we've got left in the cupboard?' *September 10*

Eight-year-old Prince William started school at £2350-a-term Ludgrove prep in Berkshire accompanied by a 'guardian angel' from Scotland Yard.

'Dammit, Sergeant Wilkins! We're supposed to be inconspicuous. Put out that ruddy pipe!' *September 11*

In the biggest military operation since the Falklands War, Britain mobilized forces from bases all over the world to fight in the 140-degree heat of the Gulf.

'For the benefit of those who didn't read Part One Orders, we put on our lightweight-issue gear AFTER we've transferred to the Gulf.' *September 12*

Lovable monster Frank N. Stein was galvanized into life in a £20 million advertising campaign to switch the public on to buying shares in the newly privatized local electricity distribution companies.

'Whatever it is, Brenda, don't go falling for any sales spiel!' *September 14*

Recuperating from a second operation on his broken right arm, the Prince of Wales missed the spectacular flypast of 166 aircraft over Buckingham Palace to mark the 50th anniversary of the Battle of Britain.

'Sorry to drag you chaps up again. Prince Charles wants it slower this time – after all, he is painting left-handed.' *September 17*

Three left-wing labour MPs flew out to Baghdad in an effort to free hostages being used as a 'human shield' by Saddam Hussein. Tory MPs warned that they were walking into an Iraqi propaganda trap.

'There are three of them going – maybe we can persuade a few more.' *September 20*

While opening a centre for holistic medicine in London, the Princess of Wales revealed that she had weekly acupuncture and Japanese massage sessions to help her relax from the stresses of royal life.

'I'm sure Princess Diana's acupuncture sessions would be even more relaxing if she could overcome her shyness.' *September 21*

Chancellor John Major delighted homeowners and City businessmen when he announced that Britain would at last join the European exchange-rate mechanism, coupling the move with a 1 per cent cut in interest rates.

'Wake up, Pickering! Things must be looking up – somebody wants to buy a house!' *October 8*

In a massive £2 million anti-terrorist operation at the Conservative Party conference in Bournemouth, 1500 police – many armed with submachine-guns – subjected delegates to extensive body and baggage searches.

'Oh come now, officer. I know them well – they haven't all got shifty eyes.' *October 9*

Transport Secretary Cecil Parkinson outlined a dynamic new programme to ease chronic congestion on Britain's roads.

'Surely you've heard of Mr Parkinson's pledge to ease congestion on our roads, sir?' *October 11*

With a rising crime rate among children living at home, there were moves were made to make parents more accountable.

'So, all those nights you were supposed to be at Cubs you were really tunnelling under the Bank of England?' *October 12*

Ex-Tory leader Edward Heath's private visit to the Gulf resulted in an agreement for the release of 50 hostages. With up to 1350 Britons still trapped, might other statesman follow his lead?

'Don't tell me, let me guess . . . Harold Wilson and James Callaghan?' *October 22*

The Princess Royal was banned from driving for a month after being caught speeding twice in a week near her home in Gloucester.

'If you can catch her, Cartwright, point out to HRH the speed limit applies to horses too.' *October 23*

Accused of profiteering during the early days of the Gulf crisis, it was a pleasant surprise when oil companies dropped pump prices at truly competitive speed as fears of a shooting war appeared to fade.

'Could you put it in a bit slower? The price might go down again at any moment.' *October 25*

As hospital waiting lists topped a record 912,000, a new report claimed that figures could be cut by up to a third if more operations were carried out as 'day surgery'.

'I think it's something to do with "day surgery" and not keeping patients in overnight after their operations . . .' *October 26*

Margaret Thatcher flew home from the EC summit in Rome in a fury having been outvoted 11–1 in favour of creating a European central bank and a single currency by the year 2000.

'Sorry, Denis. I was dreaming I was back in Rome talking to the other Common Market leaders . . .'
October 29

An experimental on-the-spot £10 fine scheme was introduced for fare-dodgers on the Fenchurch Street line. Some guilty commuters, blaming long queues at ticket offices, refused to pay.

'He refused to pay his on-the-spot fine this morning and got clamped.' *October 30*

Britain and France were united when a two-inch bore-hole 14 miles from the Kent coast joined up with the French Chunnellers, allowing through a 'whiff of garlic'. Mrs Thatcher's stance on Europe, however, cast a shadow.

'Sacre bleu! It is wet concrete! Zey have bunged up their side again!' *November 1*

In an attempt to avoid another poll-tax fiasco, Environment Secretary Chris Patten announced tough new measures for capping high-spending councils.

'Right, Item 3. Are there any suggestions how we can cut back to avoid being capped?' *November 2*

Elizabeth Taylor auctioned her treasured Van Gogh painting bought while filming *The VIPs* in London with Richard Burton. Of great sentimental value, she said she was selling it for 'entirely personal reasons'.

'Actually, Miss Taylor, when we said it would fetch more money signed, we meant by the artist.'
November 6

At the State opening of Parliament, the Queen's Speech included a statement that punishments for criminals should more closely fit their crimes. Some Tory stalwarts regarded Michael Heseltine's views as treasonable.

'Ah, Michael – anything new from Maggie in the Queen's Speech?' *November 8*

In a chilling ultimatum hinting at imminent war, Mrs Thatcher urged Saddam Hussein either to get out of Kuwait or be removed by force. 'He has been warned,' she told a hushed House of Commons.

'WARMONGERING HAG!' *November 9*

In a blitzkrieg-style media campaign for the leadership of the Conservative Party, Michael Heseltine appeared on so many TV and radio programmes that it seemed at times that he had somehow managed to clone himself.

'Okay lads, no time to lose. We've got interviews with the Press, ITV, Channel 4, BBC1, BBC2, *Wogan*, Sky, LBC . . .' *November 16*

Despite support from big-business chiefs and strong Tory constituency backing, Mrs Thatcher showed her concern for her position by launching a ferocious personal attack on Michael Heseltine.

'Hello, hello, hello – do I detect a teensy-weensy trace of anxiety?' *November 19*

Mrs Thatcher failed to win a clear victory by four votes, and immediately announced that she would be putting her name forward for the next round. In the struggle for power, the only winners seemed to be Labour.

'The fighting goes on and on! But at the end there's only one winner – a Welsh bloke with freckles.'
November 22

In a sensational turnround, Margaret Thatcher, the longest-serving Prime Minister this century, resigned. Foreign Secretary Douglas Hurd and Chancellor John Major now threw their hats into the ring.

WHO'S BIG ENOUGH? *November 23*

The Thatchers began to move family belongings into their new residence in Dulwich. Dubbed 'Dunrulin' by some neighbours, its high-security profile made it more reminiscent of Colditz.

'Honestly! I only wanted to borrow a cup of sugar!' *November 26*

All three leadership contestants claimed support from eminent Tories whilst a variety of inducements were offered to win over floating voters in the party.

'I can't make up my mind – Heseltine's offering two luscious research assistants to Major's one, but Hurd's thrown in a Caribbean cruise plus Green stamps . . .' *November 27*

At 47 John Major became Britain's youngest Prime Minister this century when Douglas Hurd and Michael Heseltine conceded defeat. The media made much of his working-class background.

'John! John! Guess what? There's a proper bath upstairs!' *November 29*

A 51-year-old Sussex vicar was sacked by a church court after being found guilty of committing adultery with two married women and making passes at a number of other parishioners.

'Thank you for all you've done, but honestly, Vicar, I can manage from now on . . .' *November 30*

Labour fears about the electability of the newly revitalized Tory Party led to speculation about Neil Kinnock's future as a leader.

'Aw, c'mon, be fair. Who shouted "Look out, behind you, Neil!"?' *December 3*

The Aga Khan lost his final appeal over 1989 Epsom Oaks winner, Aliysa,
disqualified after a dope test. In protest he took his 90 horses abroad.
Lester Piggott returned to racing in October after a five-year ban.

'. . . and with 50 yards to go it's Cauthen in the lead with Piggott hot on his heels . . .' *December 6*

As men returning from the Gulf were reunited with their families, tales of torture, miraculous escape and intriguing hideaways began to appear in the press. Meanwhile, the British winter set in.

'Of course, dear, after you've fixed the burst pipes, cleared the snow and reconnected the electricity, I'd love to hear what it was like being a hostage in Iraq.' *December 11*

Ivana Trump was awarded £12 million in a divorce case against her unfaithful property-tycoon husband as share profits soared for investors in the newly privatized electricity distribution companies.

'Who's the new man with Ivana Trump?' *December 13*

Mick Jagger and Jerry Hall's Hindu wedding ceremony on the idyllic South Sea island of Bali was declared invalid after it was discovered that they had failed to register the official legal documents.

'Okay, okay. The Hindu ceremony in Bali didn't work – but, honestly, this time I promise you'll become **Mrs Jagger.'** *December 14*

Following a slump in sales, 25,000 shops defied the law on Sunday trading in the biggest ever revolt against the 40-year-old Shops Act. Famous children's toy store Hamley's was one of many big names which participated.

'I'm sorry dear, but apparently they've restored the death penalty for opening grottoes on a Sunday.'

December 18

Buckingham Palace announced that the Prince of Wales would make a two-day morale-boosting visit to the 15,000-strong British task force in the Gulf.

'I'm sure it's him – he's just wished that cactus a happy Christmas.' *December 20*

£150,000-a-year Arsenal soccer star, Tony Adams, was sent to prison for
four months on a drink-driving charge.

'This is your cellmate, Mangler, who would've won £637,543 on the pools if you hadn't scored against Wimbledon last Saturday.' *December 21*

The uncertainty in the Gulf was resolved as the United Nations' deadline expired and Allied forces began a tremendous aerial blitz on Baghdad and other key targets. Saddam Hussein, however, remained defiant.

'ALL RIGHT, MEN – WE'RE READY!' *January 17*

As the aerial bombardment increased daily, the ground forces began to dig
in for the inevitable land battle that would follow.

'Dammit, Corporal Atkins! How many more times do you have to be told? In this country we dig
SHALLOW trenches.' *January 21*

Details of Saddam Hussein's bomb-proof bunker were revealed by the German companies that built it. Luxuriously furnished throughout – including a heated swimming-pool – it was completely isolated from the conflict above.

'. . . and so my fellow countrymen, despite our sufferings, together we will fight side-by-side to repel the infidels of Satan.' *January 22*

John Major's 'Get Saddam' campaign urged Iraqis to stage a coup. Meanwhile in Britain, *Satanic Verses* author Salman Rushdie continued to evade Muslim extremists bent on carrying out Ayatollah Khomeini's death sentence.

'Any useful tips would be most gratefully received, Mr Rushdie . . .' *January 24*

TV chiefs ignored floods of complaints about blanket coverage of the Gulf War disrupting regular programme schedules. Thames TV alone received 700 letters a day, mostly from fans of soap operas.

'. . . and now, another non-stop bombardment of repeat film clips, analysis, news and views from the Gulf . . .' *January 25*

Outrage at the war grew as the world's biggest oil slick clogged up essential water desalination plants and destroyed wildlife, particularly waterfowl, throughout the Gulf region.

January 28

The macho image of Australia's bronzed beach boys had sand kicked in its face when a survey revealed that most 'surfies' aged between 16 and 35 preferred riding the big waves to having sex.

'This sex thing, Dad. You tried it once, didn't you? What's it like?' *January 31*

Foreign Secretary Douglas Hurd flew to Bonn in a bid to win more support from Germany whose £20 million contribution to the Allied war effort was felt to be standoffish. Chancellor Kohl pledged a further £275 million.

'Apparently we simply get up early and lay them on the beach – the Germans say they're wonderful for claiming territory.' *February 1*

The Princess of Wales' brother, NBC TV reporter Viscount Althorp, admitted to an affair with cartoonist Sally Ann Lasson only six months after his marriage. Repentant, he posed for photographers with his wife and new baby.

'Frankly, if your wife can do that with a baby's rattle, how would you manage against an Iraqi with a bazooka, Viscount Althorp?' *February 4*

A survey of the world's richest women revealed that the Queen still led the field with assets of £6600 million and an estimated daily income of £1.8 million, reopening the media debate regarding her exemption from taxation.

'Philip, have you been at my purse? – I'm £1.27p short!' *February 5*

Travel companies reported a decline in American tourists in Europe following threats of terrorist retaliation by Saddam Hussein. Meanwhile, temperatures plummeted in the coldest snap for four years.

'I said, if only they could pluck up courage and get on a plane, all those American tourists would realize what they've been missing . . .' *February 11*

The *Sunday Times* attacked the younger royals for 'parading a mixture of upper-class decadence and insensitivity' with regard to the Gulf War.

'Thank you, Ma'am, but honestly, we feel the Royal Family is doing quite enough for the war effort . . .'
February 12

BR was heavily criticized when 65 per cent of trains failed due to the 'wrong type of snow'. Even the multi-million-pound InterCity 225 'super-trains' were hit when the powder-like snow blocked their air-intakes.

'No, you can't speak to the station master! Due to a design fault his air-intake has been blocked by snow.' *February 14*

The Kremlin announced that a jailed British businessman was at the centre of a 'rouble plot' to flood the USSR with currency in an attempt to cause hyperinflation and topple President Gorbachev.

'Miss Binks, have you been plotting to overthrow Mikhail Gorbachev and ruin the Soviet economy by any chance?' *February 15*

In a last-ditch bid for peace, Iraq's Foreign Minister, Tariq Aziz, was invited to Moscow. However, the Iraqis' insistence on 'linkage' to the Palestinian question and other conditions proved unacceptable.

'Mr Aziz. We'll discuss your finding a good woman and settling down safely in Moscow later – now, about Kuwait . . .' *February 18*

The Princess of Wales, like the Duchess of York, announced that she planned to 'stop at two' children.

'I think it's something to do with Princess Diana's decision not to have any more children.' *February 22*

As Allied ground troops from 10 nations poured into Kuwait, 10,000 Iraqi soldiers surrendered.

'All right, men, break it to me gently. How many troops deserted today? . . . Men?' *February 26*

209 days after being seized by Iraq, Kuwait City was free once more. As massive Allied forces pressed on towards the border, Tony Benn called for a halt to the 'brutal savagery' now that the Iraqis were withdrawing.

'Ah, cabbie. Wedgwood Benn's house, Holland Park, London – and make it snappy!' *February 28*

In a defiant broadcast after the end of hostilities, Baghdad Radio claimed the Gulf War as a glorious Iraqi triumph. Not surprisingly, there were some dissenting voices.

'I think the reason they're not cheering your God-given victory, Illustrious One, is that most of them are widows and grieving mothers . . .' *March 1*

Prime Minister John Major faced his first critical by-election test at the formerly 'safe' Tory seat of Ribble Valley. A spectacular win by the Liberal Democrats made the prospect of a June election remote.

'. . . and now, after months of non-stop analysis and debate about the war, our team of experts turn their attention to the possibility of a June election . . .' *March 4*

A magazine report revealed that the cost of getting married had risen by 10 per cent to £7359. Also, though expenditure was being increasingly shared, 68 per cent of brides' parents still paid for the nuptials themselves.

'Mummy, Daddy! Wonderful news! Rodney has just popped the question.' *March 5*

With the war over, British troops slowly began to withdraw from the Gulf.

'Terribly sad. Came through the war completely unscathed and then forgot Mother's Day . . .' *March 11*

In Birmingham, news of three women reported as having artificial insemination treatment because they had no intention of getting married or having sex with men led to a stormy debate over the ethics of virgin births.

'**Ah. That must be my order from the sperm bank.**' *March 12*

After heavy attacks by the Opposition and the prospect of a back-bench revolt, pressure built up on Environment Minister, Michael Heseltine, to find a solution to the thorny problem of the community charge.

'Yes, Michael. A pretty little aeroplane – but have you come up with anything on the poll tax yet?'
March 14

Free-range lamb bred on the Duchy of Cornwall's estates was offered for sale at some Tesco supermarkets. The Prince of Wales also approved the design for a ranch-style Tesco store on a Duchy-controlled site.

'It was designed by Prince Charles.' *March 18*

Speculation was rife as to what Chancellor Norman Lamont's budget would reveal.

'Quick! Buy ten crates! Mrs Lamont has just bought two tins of Gribley's gherkin-flavoured fish paste . . .' *March 19*

The budget speech included news that mobile phones would be taxed for the
first time.

'I had hoped that the new tax on mobile phones would stop Jeremy transacting business
during lunch . . .' *March 21*

There was public delight and considerable confusion amongst Opposition parties when the Chancellor announced that £140 would be deducted from everyone's poll tax. The paperwork, however, was another problem.

'No. Not much in the post, dear – just more poll-tax adjustments . . .' *March 22*

Veteran rock star Rod Stewart claimed that he was ready to have children with his 22-year-old bride. Meanwhile, 59-year-old entertainer Des O'Connor split up with his young Swiss wife.

'It's your lucky night, girls. I'm Des O'Connor, footloose and fancy free again and this is Rod Stewart let out for the evening . . .' *March 25*

A paternity suit filed in New Zealand against Captain Mark Phillips, estranged husband of the Princess Royal, caused problems at Buckingham Palace.

'Frankly, Mother, we feel you're worrying too much about any fresh scandals hitting the family.'
March 26

Government statistics revealed that 1990 was the most lawless year on record, 94 per cent of all crimes being against property.

'Yes madam, we are in receipt of your 999 call, but we're a little tied up at the moment . . .' *March 28*

An additional £30,000 a year was awarded to former premiers to maintain their private offices. Though ex-PMs Home, Wilson, Callaghan and Heath were also eligible, some critics felt it was 'hush money' for Mrs Thatcher.

'£30,000 for me, Prime Minister? How nice. Pop it in my "in" tray, there's a good fellow.' *March 29*

A 30-year-old woman claimed she had been raped at the Kennedy mansion after a wild night at clubs and restaurants involving Senator Edward Kennedy, his son Patrick and nephew William Kennedy Smith.

'Shucks, Mary Lou, of course you look pretty. Now have a nice time at Senator Kennedy's party.'
April 4

Young Conservative Chairman, Murdo Fraser, condemned the party's decision to abolish the poll tax. Press reports confirmed that London Zoo in Regent's Park was to close through lack of funds.

'Edward, there's a person at the door – I think it's someone from the Young Conservatives . . .' *April 8*

With the end of the Gulf War, Saddam Hussein returned to oppressing the Kurds. John Major's proposal for creating 'safe havens' for refugees attracted little attention from President Bush at first.

'Okay, Mr President, that today's fishing, golf, tennis and baseball done. Next on your agenda is the Kurdish problem . . . Mr President . . .? *April 11*

News of the World journalists claimed that Sara Dale, the 'whole-person healing therapist' occupying Chancellor Norman Lamont's former home in Notting Hill, was running a 'kinky sex parlour'.

'Whole-person healing therapist? No, as a matter of fact I'm queuing to see Norman Lamont . . .'
April 15

Home Secretary Kenneth Baker announced the start of Crime Prevention Week.

'Come out, Hetherington! This is your boss, don't think I haven't noticed the paper-clips disappearing from your office!' *April 16*

A former Highgrove policeman was paid £20,000 for a story alleging that the Prince and Princess of Wales slept in separate rooms and only saw each other at weekends.

''Ello, 'ello 'ello, what's all this 'ere, then?' *April 18*

Broadcasting rights in some of Britain's greatest sporting events were offered for sale to satellite, cable and foreign TV stations at up to five times the prices currently paid by the BBC and ITV.

'That one's for Wimbledon, that one's for the Boat Race, that one's for . . .' *April 19*

Sunday 21 April was Census Day. Every householder was legally obliged to fill in the form whether running in the ADT London Marathon or not.

'Here comes your dad now. Wait till he hears he's got a £400 fine for not filling in the Census form last night.' *April 22*

'That's a promise, Dr Owen – if your talks with the Tory Party come to nothing, we'll think about it.'

April 23

The Tories' proposed new 'council tax', devised to replace the community charge, would introduce a flat-rate tax based on the market value of a property with a 25 per cent discount for people living alone.

'Same here. Everything was fine until he read the bit about people living alone getting a 25 per cent discount.'
April 25

In the aftermath of the Guildford Four and Birmingham Six cases, public opinion of the police force hit an all-time low. Official statistics showed that complaints had soared to an average of 137 per week.

'Personally, I think the Chief is over-reacting to all these complaints against the police.' *April 26*

Black rights campaigner Rev. Al Sharpton arrived in Britain to tour
Brixton, Toxteth and other race hot-spots. Meanwhile, H.E. Bates' comedy,
The Darling Buds of May, continued to top the ratings on ITV.

'I'm sorry we missed throwing off the shackles of White oppression last night, Reverend – *The Darling Buds of May* was on.' *April 29*

British plans to send a lightly armed European force into Iraq to replace Allied troops protecting the Kurds' 'safe havens' won backing from the EC in Luxemburg.

'Right, chaps. Some of you may be wondering why we're not using our normal patrol cars today.'

April 30

MPs decided to bypass the House of Lords, which had voted against a proposed War Crimes Bill allowing prosecution of alleged Nazi war criminals living in Britain. In the local elections, the Conservatives again fared badly.

'You heard, Schweinhund! Before voting I vant to know your stance on ze war crimes issue!' *May 2*

Research showed that motorists under 20 were up to four times more likely to be involved in accidents than others. Tougher L-tests, stricter drinking laws and one-year 'probation plates' were suggested to combat the problem.

'Congratulations, young man – you can throw away those L-plates now.' *May 3*

Thousands of stay-at-home trippers flocked to their local DIY stores on a damp May Bank Holiday as the High Court lifted local council Sunday-trading bans on B&Q and other shops.

'It's about yesterday's service, Vicar. And your prayer for lightning, hellfire and torment to smite the Philistines at B & Q's store down the road.' *May 6*

The Princess of Wales saw little of her husband during the royal visit to Czechoslovakia – not only did they sleep in separate rooms on different floors in Prague Castle but they also had separate official engagements.

'Bad news, darling, I think my wife's beginning to suspect – she's insisted on separate apartments . . .'
May 7

An industrial tribunal ruled in favour of a butler and his 'plain Yorkshire cooking' wife who had been unfairly dismissed. The butler said he saw his wife's replacement pour a £500 bottle of Château Lafite into the goulash.

'At least with Tomkiss, we know he'd never allow our best wine to be put in the goulash.' *May 9*

Neil Kinnock fired his electoral starting gun by stating that under Labour there would be no tax cuts for five years and that the National Insurance contributions ceiling would be abolished. Had he shot himself in the foot?

'. . . and furthermore, we'll bleed you dry – you fat, go-getting, wealth-creating git! . . . I do hope we can count on your support.' *May 10*

Three-foot octopuses capable of delivering a nasty bite invaded the south coast following a population explosion. Meanwhile, particularly vicious attacks on children by pit bull terriers led to an import ban.

"Ere, that's nice, Sid – I've been lookin' for somethin' to replace my pit bull terrier.' *May 28*

Transport Secretary Malcolm Rifkind announced that haulage contractors would be offered big cash incentives to switch juggernaut freight from road to rail.

"Tis all right Rifkind sayin' everythin's got to go by rail – he doesn't have to balance this ruddy lorry!'
May 30

Further legislation was introduced to curb aggressive fighting dogs. News also leaked out of scandalous conditions in Staffordshire children's homes employing the ruthless 'Pin-down' confinement regime.

'Bad news – he's to be muzzled, neutered and do six months' solitary at a Staffordshire children's home.' *May 31*

'Oh no, not again! Dammit, Maggie, must you pack every time Major gets a bad opinion poll?' *June 3*

As more small businesses went bust, outrage at exorbitant charges by High Street banks, despite a fall in base interest rates, led to a major inquiry by the Treasury.

'Give him the money, Hoskins. We are in the same business after all . . .' *June 4*

'Only got time for four courses today, Pilbeam. We're debating Waldegrave's health proposals in half an hour.' *June 6*

A computerized fingerprinting scheme was proposed to crack down on illegal immigrants falsely claiming political asylum in Britain. Cross-party support was also given to the muzzling and neutering of dangerous dogs.

'A slight misunderstanding, sir. We only want your fingerprints – you don't have to be neutered and muzzled.' *June 11*

Further anti-EC statements from the Tory Bruges Group led John Major to deliver two powerful broadsides. *The Silence of the Lambs*, a film about a psychopath so dangerous he has to wear a face mask, was a box-office smash.

'Psst, Percy, old boy. What's this "Silence of the Lambs" the PM keeps muttering about?' *June 14*

Dr Roger Billings hit the headlines with an electric-powered Ford Fiesta whose motor extracted hydrogen from water. Oil companies worldwide received the news with concern.

'Next item on the agenda. What action should illustrious members take over the news that some infidel has invented a car that runs on water . . .?' *June 18*

Torrential rain put paid to cricket as well as most other sports.

'and a ripple of excitement runs through the crowd as the umpires go out to inspect the pitch . . .'
June 25

John Major condemned massive pay rises of more than eight times the rate of inflation by bosses of newly privatized companies. The salary of National Power's chief executive had leapt 58 per cent to £135,000.

'Miss Jones, look through the dictionary, will you – what does "recession" mean?' *June 27*

Patrick Pottle and Michael Randle, who had helped Soviet master spy George Blake escape from prison 25 years ago and published a book about it, were acquitted by an Old Bailey jury.

'I was bored, dear. So I thought, why not break into Wormwood Scrubs, free a few prisoners, then write a book?' *June 28*

The Princess of Wales spent her 30th birthday alone in London as Prince Charles remained at Highgrove nursing a painful back. Romantics hoped for a surprise appearance at an informal dinner for friends in the evening.

'Oh, I say, I'm terribly sorry! One seems to have been delivered to the wrong address . . .' *July 1*

Thames Water supremo Roy Watts nearly doubled his salary in what Labour critics labelled an act of 'sheer unbridled greed'. It looked like being the wettest July for decades.

'People may criticize him, but I think he's doing a wonderful job . . .' *July 2*

There was a public outcry when two IRA suspecs escaped from Brixton Prison using a semi-automatic pistol somehow smuggled past the guards.

'I was hoping to smuggle in the last bit for your Centurion tank, but they've tightened up on security suddenly.' *July 8*

'You've got to remember, they've been waiting 30 years for this.' *July 11*

Facing economic disaster and political turmoil at home, Soviet President Gorbachev pleaded for aid from the world's most powerful industrial nations meeting in London for the G7 summit.

'Simpson, the person you found standing outside with a begging bowl is not Mr Gorbachev!' *July 15*

A Department of the Environment inquiry was launched after millions of gallons of untreated water were pumped into homes in the Rickmansworth area following a breakdown at the Three Valleys Water Services company.

'The water company says it's all right as long as you don't drink it . . .' *July 22*

Moves towards Western-style democracy in the USSR were attacked by old-guard Communists who urged a coup against President Gorbachev. At home, cutbacks in some prestigious Army regiments led to ill-feeling.

'Norma, come quickly – the Soviet army is being urged to stage a coup against Gorbachev . . .' *July 25*

In a final bid to oust Militant supporters, two Labour MPs were ordered to explain their political affiliations to the party's National Executive Committee.

'Always happens – summer recess, no cameras, no microphones or witnesses – one of them'll pop out of the closet . . .' *July 26*

Over 120,000 people attended an open-air concert in Hyde Park to celebrate
Luciano Pavarotti's 30 years as an opera star.

'Sure, honey . . . for £300 we got darned good seats – but I've always thought Pavarotti was a big guy
with a beard.' *July 30*